Gregory's Mediterranean Cuisine
Recipes of Albania, Macedonia, Croatia, Turkey, and Greece

By

Dr. Gregory Evangelos Zotos Ph.D.

PublishAmerica
Baltimore

First printing

At the specific preference of the author, PublishAmerica allowed this work to remain exactly as the author intended, verbatim, without editorial input.

ISBN: 1-4241-3022-0
PUBLISHED BY PUBLISHAMERICA, LLLP
www.publishamerica.com
Baltimore

Printed in the United States of America

I would like to dedicate this book to my magnificent mother Cathy Zotos, who has enhanced my life by the glow of her love. To my late father Evangelos Zotos and my late sister Connie Zotos, who will always be angels in my heart. In addition, to my Yia Yia and Papou (Grandmother and Grandfather), whose inspiration and love have been so valuable to my life.

Acknowledgments

I would like to acknowledge the entire staff of PublishAmerica for giving my books a chance to be published. I thank the entire staff from the bottom of my heart.

Everyone who purchased my first two books "Gregory's Pita Pocket Full of Simple Greek Recipes" and "Gregory's Greek Kitchen." The media, booksellers, stores, internet sites, newspapers, and supporters, I thank you from the bottom of my heart.

ΕΥΧΑΡΙΣΤΟ

THANK YOU

Author's Notes

If you loved *Gregory's Pita Pocket Full of Simple Greek Recipes* and *Gregory's Greek Kitchen,* my first two Greek recipe books, you will savor this new book I have prepared. Gregory's Mediterranean Cuisine offers you the opportunity to prepare and savor mouth-watering old recipes and some very new recipes that were made in the old towns in Albania, Macedonia, Croatia, Turkey, and Greece. I have put together a wonderful collection of recipes of Albania, Macedonia, Croatia, Turkey, and Greece that I have made very simple and easy to make. The mouth-watering tastes of Albania, Macedonia, Croatia, Turkey, and Greece will lie ahead for buyers of this book.

It is particularly difficult to locate a Albanian, Macedonian, Croatian, Turkish, and Greek cookbook that grabs hold of the old village recipes that have that exceptional Albanian, Macedonian, Croatian, Turkish, and Greek taste one can get only by the groundwork in the old towns. I have secured this in my recipe book. I would like to tender others the chance to buy my exceptional book and to be able to be subjected to simple, fun, Albanian, Macedonian, Croatian, Turkish, and Greek recipes.

NOTES

I have incorporated a portion of each page labeled "cooking notes" following every recipe. This page is a very effective tool for everyone to utilize. When you are cooking and you perhaps do not want the recipe as spicy the next time you make it, you may jot this type of note down under the cooking instructions. This way the next time you cook it, you will remember that helpful hint.

Oven temperatures vary. Another helpful cooking note may be if a recipe gets done earlier than stated, your oven temperature is a little different. Please note this in the cooking instructions for future use.

Albania Recipes Section

Albania Lamb with Yogurt—Taavee koosii

- ½ cup of Feta Cheese
- 4 pounds leg of lamb
- 4 jumbo eggs beaten
- 1 tablespoon flour
- 1 cup yogurt
- ¾ cup butter
- 2 tablespoons rice
- ½ cup of minced garlic
- Salt
- pepper
- ½ cup of dill weed

Bake the leg of lamb in a greased baking pan at 375 degrees for 30 minutes or until brown. Remove the leg of lamb pan from the oven and let sit. Mix all of the ingredients together in a mixing bowl and mix well. Salt and pepper should be added to the mixture by adding 3 pinches of salt and 3 pinches of pepper to taste. Pour mixture over the leg of lamb and bake at 350 degrees 3 hours or until done to your consistency.

COOKING NOTES:

Albania Salad

- ¾ cup of extra virgin olive oil
- 1 cup of chopped onions
- ½ cup of dill weed
- 1 cup of Feta Cheese
- 1 head of lettuce
- ½ cup of lemon juice
- salt
- pepper
- 4 sliced hard boiled eggs

Clean and tear up lettuce into pieces and put in a large bowl. Add each ingredient to the lettuce and mix well so as much of each ingredient is spread throughout the bowl. Add salt and pepper to taste.

COOKING NOTES:

Albania Tuna Steak

- ¼ cup of Dill weed
- ¾ tsp. fresh squeezed lemon
- 1 tbsp. flour
- ¼ cup of crumbled Feta Cheese
- ¾ cup of white wine
- 1 1/2 lb tuna
- ½ cup chopped onion
- ½ tsp rosemary
- ¾ tbsp butter

Combine all of the ingredients in a mixing bowl and mix very well. Be sure that the tuna is completely covered with all the ingredients well. Let marinade for 3 hours. Put in a baking pan and bake for 350 for 45 minutes or until crumbling appears on top of the fish.

COOKING NOTES:

Albania Dry Fig Delight

- ½ cup chocolate chips
- ¾ cup of sugar
- 4 cups milk
- 11/4 cups thinly shredded fresh figs green

Combine the milk and sugar mixture in a medium height pan and bring to a boil. Turn off heat and combine the figs. Pour into cupcake holders in cupcake pan. Bake at 325 degrees for 11 minutes or until golden brown. Put in refrigerator and let harden. After hardening, put some chocolate chips over the top of each one. Enjoy!

COOKING NOTES:

Albania Roast Lamb

- ¼ cup of Feta Cheese
- ½ cup of minced garlic
- 1 lamb roast about six ribs
- 1 tsp salt
- 1/3 tsp ground black pepper
- ¼ cup of oregano

Mix all of the ingredients together in a mixing bowl. Mix well. Place lamb into mixing bowl and put all mixed ingredients all over the lamb. The more you distribute all over the lamb, the better the taste will be. Transfer the seasoned lamb to a 9 X 13 greased pan. Set oven to bake at 350 degrees. Roast for 1 hour or until brown.

COOKING NOTES:

Albania Halvah

- ½ cup of chopped pecans
- ½ cup of flour
- ¼ cup of butter
- 1 cup water
- 1 tbsp lime juice
- ¼ cup of sugar

Combine water, lime juice and sugar in a stove top pan and bring to a boil. In another pan melt the butter. When the butter has melted, add to the other pan with the boiled ingredients. Add in pecans and flour.

COOKING NOTES:

Albania Brown Meatballs—Qooftee ta Feerguaaraa

- ¼ cup of crumbled Feta cheese
- ¼ cup flour
- ¼ cup of dill weed
- ½ pound of ground lamb
- ¾ cup of extra virgin olive oil
- ¼ cup of crumbled Kasseri cheese
- ¼ cup of onion
- Pinch of salt
- ¼ cup of bread crumbs
- Pinch of pepper

Mix all of the ingredients together except for the flour and extra virgin olive oil in a large mixing bowl. Be sure that the lamb is mixed very well with all of the ingredients. Take the mixture and form into medium sized meatballs. Sprinkle flour all over the meatballs. Bake at 335 degrees in the extra virgin olive oil for 1 hour or until brown.

COOKING NOTES:

Albania Cabbage and Potato Soup

- 2 tbsp. of Red wine
- ½ pound chopped cabbage
- ¼ cup of dill weed
- ½ pound chopped potatoes
- ¼ cup of feta cheese
- 2 tbsp butter
- ½ cup onion
- 1 tbsp flour
- ½ cup carrots
- pinch of salt
- ¼ cup of chopped tomatoes
- pinch of pepper

Combine all of the ingredients together mix well in a tall pan. Bring to a boil. Simmer until potatoes and carrots are soft. Let stand for 8 minutes to allow ingredients to set for best taste.

COOKING NOTES:

Albania Brown Meatballs—Qooftee tee Feerguaaraa

- ¼ cup of oregano
- ¼ cup of Kasseri cheese
- ½ pound ground lamb
- 1 slice hard bread
- salt
- pepper
- 1 cup Extra virgin olive oil
- ¾ cup of chopped onion

Combine all of the ingredients together except for the slice of hard bread. Mix ingredients well. Take slice of hard bread and place in a soup bowl with water. Let soften. Take the soft pieces and combine into the mixture. Mix very well. Take a small bunch of the mixture and form into meatballs. Fry in medium heat until brown.

COOKING NOTES:

Albania Small Hambugers—Qaafteee

- ½ cup of dill weed
- 11/2lbs. ground lamb
- ½ cup of Kasseri cheese
- 2 small eggs
- ¼ cup of chopped onions
- 1 cup of breadcrumbs
- ½ cup of pitless Kalamata Olives
- 1 cup of minced garlic
- ½ cup of Feta Cheese

Combine all of the ingredients together in a mixing bowl. Mix very well for the best flavor and taste. Shape into small hamburger patties and bake at 350 degrees until preferred consistency or brown.

COOKING NOTES:

Turkish Recipes Section

Turkish Kuuftaa

- 1 cup of tomato sauce
- ½ cup of minced garlic
- 1 3/4 pounds of Lamb
- ¼ cup of feta cheese
- pinch of salt
- pinch of pepper
- 3 sliced potatoes
- ¼ cup of dill weed

Combine all of the ingredients together except for the potatoes and tomatoes and mix well. Now take the combined ingredients that are mixed well and put them in a greased 9 x 13 pan. Set oven to broil and broil until brown color appears. Remove. Sprinkle potatoes and tomatoes over the entire top of the food. Now bake 350 degrees for 55 minutes.

COOKING NOTES:

Turkish Sea Bass

½ cup of minced garlic
½ cup of Feta cheese
½ cup Kasseri cheese
½ cup of dill weed
1 ½ tsp salt
½ cup of white wine
1 ½ pound whole sea bass (cleaned)
½ cup of extra virgin olive oil
2 tsp pepper

Combine all of the ingredients except for the sea bass. Mix very well. Pour mixed ingredients in a 9x13 pan. Put the sea bass in the pan and be sure all of the ingredients are spread over and under the sea bass for best taste. Bake in oven at 350 for 30 minutes or until fish is flaky.

COOKING NOTES:

Turkish Soup

- ¼ cup oregano
- ½ pound of beef
- ¼ cup butter
- 2 cups of bottled water
- 2 tbsp salt
- 1 cup flour
- ¼ cup feta cheese

Combine all of the ingredients in a tall pan. Mix well. Bring to a boil or until beef is brown and cooked well. Stir on occasion, so all will mix well.

COOKING NOTES:

Turkish Cream Tomatoes

- ¼ cup of Feta cheese
- ¾ cup of warm milk
- 3 large tomatoes
- ¼ cup of butter
- 1 fresh squeezed lemon
- pinch of salt
- pinch of pepper
- ¼ cup of oregano
- ½ cup of flour

Place the tomatoes in a pan on the stove and put on medium heat. Cook each side of the tomatoes until they turn brown. Combine all of the other ingredients together and mix. Now add the cooked tomatoes. Pour in a tall pan, put on medium heat and stir constantly until it comes to a boil. Let set for a couple of minutes and serve warm.

COOKING NOTES:

Turkish Garlic/Yogurt Topping— Haaydaarii

- ¼ cut minced garlic
- 5 cups yogurt
- 1 teaspoon pepper
- salt to taste
- ¼ cup of extra virgin olive oil
- ¼ cup oregano
- ¼ cup of hot peppers
- ¼ cup of dill weed

Remove any liquid in the yogurt. Mix all of the ingredients together and mix well. Stir until soft. Put in the refrigerator and semi-freeze or chill. When semi-frozen serve or chilled serve.

COOKING NOTES:

Turkish Leeks

- 1/3 cup of elbow macaroni
- 1 ½ pound of fresh leeks
- 1 ¾ cup of water
- ½ cup of Extra Virgin Olive Oil
- ¼ cup of lemon juice
- ½ cup of Feta Cheese
- 1 stalk of Celery
- 1 ½ tsp. Sugar
- ¼ cup of oregano
- ½ tsp salt

Leeks should be cleaned and soft layers kept. Combine all of the ingredients except the elbow macaroni together and mix well. Put in a tall pan and simmer for 50 minutes on medium heat, or until a creamy look appears. At the end of 30 minutes, add the elbow macaroni.

COOKING NOTES:

Turkish Yogurt Soup

- ¼ cup of dill weed
- ¼ cup sugar
- 7 cups of water
- 1/3 cup of flour
- cinnamon to taste
- 3 egg yolks
- salt to taste
- 2 3/4 cups yogurt
- ¼ cup of butter
- 1/4 cup rice

In large mixing bowl mix all of the ingredients together except the water and the rice. Mix very well. In a tall pan cook the rice and water for about 15 minutes on medium heat, mixing as it cooks. When completely cooked add the mixed ingredients to the pan of cooked rice and water. Mix very well. Stir constantly and put on low heat for about 12 minutes or until a smooth texture appears. Put in soup bowls and serve.

COOKING NOTES:

Turkish Fruit dish—Hooshaaf

- ¼ cup chopped walnuts
- 7 seedless grapes
- 13 slices Dried apples
- 15 slices Dried pears
- 7 small Dried apricots
- 1/3 cup Raisins
- 3 cups Water
- 1/4 cup strawberry molasses

Combine all of the ingredients together except for the molasses. Let set for 8 hours. Pour in a tall pan and boil low for 35 minutes. Let cool. Put in bowls and put in the refrigerator to chill. Serve cold and enjoy.

COOKING NOTES:

Turkish Peppers and Eggplant—Aajvaarr

- ¼ cup of dill weed
- 2 small chopped hot peppers
- 3 sliced large eggplants
- ¼ cup chopped peppers
- 1 fresh squeezed lemon
- pinch of salt
- pinch of pepper
- 1 cup of extra virgin olive oil
- 2 cups of water
- ½ cup of minced garlic

Combine all of the ingredients except the peppers and eggplant and mix well. Place the peppers and eggplant in a pan on the stove and put on medium heat. Cook each side of the eggplant and pepper until they turn brown. Add to the rest of the mix ingredients. Mix well. Put in a tall pan and bring to a boil. Let simmer for 8 minutes and serve.

COOKING NOTES:

Turkish Lamb Dish

- ¼ cup dill weed
- 1 cup chopped carrots
- 1 cup chopped celery
- 11/2 cup chopped onions
- 1 cup flour
- 1 pound cut cubed lamb shoulder
- 3 egg yolks
- 1 teaspoon butter
- ¾ cup green beans
- salt to taste
- Pepper to taste
- 3 cups water
- 1 cup yogurt
- ½ cup Feta cheese

Mix all of the ingredients together except for the butter and lamb shoulder. Mix very well. Cook the lamb shoulder in the butter on bake 300 degrees for 10 minutes. Remove any excess material in the pan after cooking. Now add the remaining ingredients. Cook for approximately 1¾ hours or until golden brown and lamb is cooked.

COOKING NOTES:

Croatian Recipes Section

Croatian Calamari with Potato—Liignjees Kruumpiroom

- 1 cup chopped Carrots
- ½ cup Extra Virgin Olive Oil
- ¼ cup of Dill Weed
- 1 pound of Calamari
- 3 pounds sliced potatoes
- ¼ cup of Oregano
- Salt to taste
- Pepper to taste
- ½ cup minced Garlic

Take long Calamari, clean very well and slice into circles. Mix all of the ingredients in a mixing bowl very well. Put in a 9 x 11 greased pan. Cover with aluminum foil. Put in oven and bake at 300 degrees for approximately 1 hour or until small bubbles arise. Check this by carefully lifting the aluminum foil.

COOKING NOTES:

Croatian Pancakes with Cottage Cheese— Faalaaciinke Caa Ciiroom

- 1/8 cup Feta Cheese
- 1/8 cup of limejuice
- 3 cups flour
- ½ cup milk
- ½ cup water
- 1 egg
- 1 teaspoon salt
- ½ cup of Extra Virgin Olive Oil
- 1/8 cup of orange juice

Mix all of the ingredients together in a large bowl. When a doughy mixture occurs, take a small part of dough and flatten into a pancake. Put some of the filling (Croatian Pancakes with cottage cheese— Faalaaciinke Caa Ciiroom—Filling in this book) in the center of the dough. Put another layer of dough over this. Roll into a tube form. Bake on a 9 x 13 pan in the oven for 30 minutes on 300 degrees or until golden brown.

COOKING NOTES:

Croatian Pancakes with Cottage Cheese— Faalaaciinke Caa Ciiroom—Filling

- 1 ¼ cups sour cream
- 2 eggs
- 2 Tbsp sugar
- 1 Tbsp dried apricots
- 1 Tbsp. dried peaches
- 1 Tbsp. dried oranges
- 1 1/4 cup large curd cottage cheese

Combine all of the ingredients together and mix very well. See previous recipe for instructions on inserting into pancakes and cooking.

COOKING NOTES:

Croatian Tomato and Onion Salad

- ½ cup of Extra Virgin Olive oil
- 1/8 cup of red wine vinegar
- 6 cups of cubed tomatoes
- 2 large sliced onions
- Salt to taste
- Pepper to taste
- ½ cup of crumbled Feta Cheese

Combine all of the ingredients in a bowl. The key here is to mix it well so all of the ingredients are evenly distributed in the salad for the best taste.

COOKING NOTES:

Croatian Doughnut Delights—Prikle

- ¼ cup Metaxa liquor
- 2 tsp. orange juice
- 4 ¾ cups flour
- ¼ cup milk
- 2 tsp. vanilla extract
- 3 eggs
- ½ cup warm water
- 1 tsp. salt
- 3 tsp. brown sugar
- 1 ½ pkgs. Dry yeast
- ¼ tsp. ground nutmeg
- ½ tsp. ground cinnamon
- 1 cup apricots

Mix all of the ingredients together in a mixing bowl. Mix extremely well. When the mixture loosens well from the bowl, cover the bowl with a wet, squeezed –out piece of paper towel. Let stand for 10 minutes. Take a clump of the mixture and shape into a small ball. Continue until all of the mixture is utilized. Deep fry balls at 300 degrees until a hard, doughnut crust appears around each of the small balls.

COOKING NOTES:

Croatian Giibaanicaa

- 1/3 cup of finely ground almonds
- 7 cups of flour
- 1 teaspoon orange juice
- ¼ cup of sugar
- 1 teaspoon salt
- ½ cup of sour cream
- 11/2 cups of milk
- 2 egg yolks
- 1/3 pound of butter
- 1 packet yeast

Mix all the ingredient together in a mixing bowl. Knead the dough mixture well. Take the dough and shape it into a long log shape. Let the dough rise in a greased pan, in a cold oven until it enlarges to about twice its size. The dough will be spongy. Stuff and cook according to the directions in my "Croatian Giibaanicaa-Stuffing" recipe in this book.

COOKING NOTES:

Croatian Giibaanicaa—Stuffing

- 2 cups of chopped walnuts
- 2 cups chopped pecans
- 3 egg whites
- ¾ cup sugar
- 1 teaspoon vanilla extract
- 1 ¼ cups cream
- ¼ cup butter
- 1 ½ tablespoons pure maple syrup
- 1/3 cup of orange juice

Combine all the ingredients together and mix well. The mixture must be well combined for the best taste. Now take the dough from the "Croatian Giibaanicaa" recipe in this book and spread the dough out. Put the stuffing on the dough and spread evenly. Now take a greased bread pan and put the dough in a log shaped with the stuffing inside and the dough rolled around it into a log. Place this in a cold oven for 50 minutes. Then turn on the oven and bake at 350 degrees for 50 minutes or until golden brown. Watch so the filling does not leak out. This means it is over cooked.

COOKING NOTES:

Croatian Stuffed Peppers

- ¾ cup Feta Cheese
- 8 large peppers
- 1 lb. ground lamb
- 1 cup chopped Hickory ham
- 1 cup chopped Hickory Bacon
- ½ cup dill weed
- 8 tbsp. flour
- 1 cups uncooked rice
- 3 eggs
- ½ cup extra virgin olive oil
- salt to taste
- Pepper to taste
- 1 cup chopped onion

Combine all the ingredients except the bacon and the peppers together in a large bowl and mix well. Fry the bacon. Add bacon to the mixture and mix well. Utilize a large 9 x 13 greased pan. Wash the peppers well. Cut the tops off in the center top of the pepper. Place the mixture evenly in each of the peppers. Put the tops back on the peppers. Bake in oven for 1 hour at 350 degrees or until the peppers begin to soften well.

COOKING NOTES:

Croatian Oookruuglii Rrrsaaak

- 1 ½ cup butter
- 1 tablespoon pecan syrup
- 16 oz confection sugar
- ¾ cup of chopped pecans
- ¼ cup of chopped Almonds
- ¼ cup of chopped walnuts
- 5 eggs
- ½ tsp. Salt
- 1 tablespoon vanilla
- 3 ¾ cups flour
- 1 tablespoon baking powder
- ¼ cup orange juice

Combine all the ingredients in a bowl and mix well until a soft mixture occurs. Put in a bread pan and bake at 300 degrees for 1 ½ hours or until golden brown.

COOKING NOTES:

Croatian Sausage, Carrots, and Potato Dish

- ½ cup onions
- 1 ½ pounds sausage
- ¼ pound bacon
- ½ cup minced garlic
- salt to taste
- pepper to taste
- ¼ cup oregano
- ¼ cup of dill weed
- ¼ cup flour
- 3 cups of bottled water
- ¼ cup of crumbled feta cheese
- 1 tablespoon vegetable seasoning
- 2 large peeled sliced Potatoes
- 2 large cubed Carrots

Mix all of the ingredients except the water in a mixing bowl mix well. Take a tall pan and pour the bottled water into the pan. Place all of the ingredients that have been mixed well into the water. Boil carefully viewing the potatoes until the potatoes become soft. At this point you know the dish is done when the potatoes become soft.

COOKING NOTES:

Macedonian Recipes
Section

Macedonian Piiinjuuur

- ½ cup of minced Garlic
- 1 large eggplant
- 1/8 cup lemon juice
- salt to taste
- ¼ cup of pitless kalamata Olives
- ½ Cup Extra Virgin Olive Oil
- 1/8 cup orange juice
- ¼ cup of Feta Cheese

Wash eggplants very well and poke holes into the eggplants. Put eggplants on a greased 9x 13 pan. Bake on 350 degrees for 25 minutes or until the eggplants fall over.

In a mixing bowl mix all of the ingredients together. When the mixture appears to be soft place some on each of the eggplants and serve.

COOKING NOTES:

Macedonia Specialty Salad

- 1 ½ cups of chopped cucumber
- 2 small eggplants
- 2 cups of sliced tomatoes
- chopped parsley
- 1 cup of chopped green pepper
- 2 scallions
- 1 sweet red pepper

First prepare the "Macedonia Specialty Salad dressing" located in this book. Combine all of the ingredients together in a mixing bowl except for the eggplant. Toss well. Clean and peel the eggplant well. Broil the eggplant low until golden brown color appears on both sides. Cut into small square- shaped pieces. Now add the eggplant to the mixture. Pour the dressing over the salad and cover as much of every single piece of the salad for the best taste.

COOKING NOTES:

Macedonia Specialty Salad Dressing

* ½ cup minced garlic
* ¼ cup of red wine
* ¼ cup of lemon
* ½ cup of Red Wine Vinegar
* salt to taste
* Pepper to taste
* ¼ cup of dill weed
* ¼ cup of crumbled Feta Cheese

Mix all of the ingredients well in a large measuring cup. The more you stir and mix the mixture, the better the taste. Utilize the measuring cup's spout for pouring onto the "Macedonian Specialty Salad "recipe found in this book.

COOKING NOTES:

Macedonian Chicken and Rice

- ¼ cup of dill weed
- 7 cups water
- ½ cup of minced garlic
- 2 ¼ cups rice
- 1 ½ pounds of chicken breasts cut up
- Salt and pepper to taste
- ¼ cup butter
- ½ cup of sliced onions
- ¼ cup of feta cheese
- ¼ cup of carrots

Cook rice according to the directions on the package. Put the water, cucumbers, onions, and carrots and chicken into a tall pan. Bring to a boil and cook until chicken and vegetables are tender. Combine all the other ingredients together and mix well in a large mixing bowl. Drain the chicken and vegetables and place in dishes. Put the mixed ingredients from the large mixing bowl over the chicken.

COOKING NOTES:

Macedonian Buffalo Chicken Wings

- 1 cup bread crumbs
- 1/8 cup dill weed
- 12 Chicken Wings
- ¼ cup Butter
- 1/8 cup minced garlic
- salt to taste
- pepper to taste

Combine all of the ingredients together except for the chicken wings and the butter. Mix the ingredients well. Take a chicken wing, and brush some butter on it. Then, dip into the ingredients mixture. Repeat until all of the wings are done. Put the completed chicken wings on a 9 x 13 greased pan. Bake at 350 for 30 minutes or until golden brown and tender.

COOKING NOTES:

Macedonian Syrup Cake—Syrup

- 1 teaspoon orange juice
- 2 ½ cups of sugar
- 4 cups of bottled water
- 1 tablespoon vanilla essence

Combine all of the ingredients together and put them in a mid-height pan. Bring to a boil and boil for 3 minutes.

COOKING NOTES:

Macedonian Syrup Cake

- 1 cup chopped pecans
- 1 ¼ cup sugar
- 1 ¼ cup butter
- 2 ¼ cups semolina
- 6 eggs
- 1 ¼ cup of flour-self rising is the best
- 1/8 cup of orange juice

Combine all of the ingredients together in a mixing bowl. Mix thoroughly. Pour into a 9 x 13 greased pan and bake for 60 minutes at 375 degrees. When cooking is complete, use a knife and cut into squares. Now take the syrup from the "Macedonian syrup cake-syrup" recipe in this book and pour over the hot squares.

COOKING NOTES:

Macedonian Traditional Small Town Salad

- 1 cup of sliced cucumbers
- 1 cup of sliced onions
- ½ cup of oregano
- ¼ cup of salt
- ¼ cup of pepper
- 1 cup sliced tomatoes
- ½ cup Extra Virgin Olive oil
- ¼ cup of Red Wine Vinegar
- ½ cup of yogurt

Combine all of the ingredients together except for the yogurt. Mix very well. Put in a salad dish and put the yogurt over the top of the salad.

COOKING NOTES:

Macedonian Stuffed Red Peppers

- 6 large red peppers
- ¼ cup of dill weed
- ½ cup of chopped onions
- ½ cup of chopped potatoes
- ¼ cup of minced garlic
- 1 ½ cup of rice
- 1 cup tomato juice
- 1 ¼ cups of Extra Virgin Olive Oil

Take the red peppers and wash outer layer. Then carefully cut the tops off straight across so about ½ inch of the skin is present from the stem. Clean out the insides of the peppers and then wash being careful not to split the peppers. Now mix the rest of the ingredients together in a mixing bowl. Scoop out some of the mixture and put inside of the pepper, repeat until all peppers have the same amount of mixture or about ¾ of the way full in each pepper. Put the tops back on the peppers. Bake in the oven at 350 degrees for approximately 1 hour or until lightly golden brown.

COOKING NOTES:

Macedonian Spaghetti and Tuna

- ½ cup of Minced Garlic
- ½ cup of Extra Virgin Olive Oil
- ¼ cup of kasseri cheese
- 1 lb spaghetti
- 1 cups of sliced Tomatoes
- ¼ cup of Oregano
- ¼ cup of dill weed
- Salt to taste
- Pepper to taste
- 2 cans of Drained Albacore Tuna

Cook the spaghetti according to the directions on the spaghetti container and drain. Mix all of the ingredients except for the spaghetti together in a mixing bowl very well. Put the spaghetti in a large serving bowl. Add the mixed ingredients to the spaghetti and mix into the spaghetti.

COOKING NOTES:

Greek Recipes Section

Greek Easter Bread—Tsoureki

- 2 packets Quick rising yeast
- 1 tbs. cranberry juice
- 2 ¼ cups of milk
- 1 ¼ cups of sugar
- ¼ cup of butter
- 7 eggs
- 2 tsp. salt
- 1 hard boiled red dyed egg
- ¼ cup sesame seeds
- 11 cups of Flour
- ½ cup of Bottled water

Combine all of the ingredients together in a mixing bowl except the sesame seeds, and hard boiled egg. Mix well. Knead the doughy mixture well. Place in a greased 9 X 13 pan. Cover with a towel and put in cold oven to rise for 1 ¾ hours. Break up the dough and roll into rope like pieces. Criss cross the ropes to form numerous figure eights. Take the hard boiled red dyed egg and place in the center. Return to cold oven, cover with towel and let rise for ¾ hours. Now remove the towel and bake at 375 degrees for 1 hour or until golden brown.

COOKING NOTES:

Greek Octopus—Ahhktaapothee Veraastou

- 1 whole Octopus
- ¼ cup of Feta Cheese
- 4 cups of water
- ¼ cup of minced garlic
- ¾ cup of Extra Virgin Olive Oil
- ¼ cup of Vinegar
- ¼ cup of Dill weed
- salt to taste
- pepper to taste

Take the octopus and clean and rinse it well. Put into a tall pan and boil until the octopus becomes tender or a dark pink color occurs. Remove octopus and peel off outer skin. Dice into 1 inch pieces. Mix all the ingredients together well in a large bowl. Cover bowl. Put into refrigerator and let marinate for 24 to 48 hours. Enjoy.

COOKING NOTES:

Greek Olive Bread—Ellies Psomee

- ¼ cup of chopped onions
- ¼ cup crumbled Feta Cheese
- 2 cups Kalamata Olives (Remove Pits)
- 1 ½ tbsp. salt
- 1/8 cup of Extra Virgin Olive Oil
- 1 ½ cup of bottled water
- 4 cups of flour
- 1 packets of rapid rise yeast
- 1/8 cup oregano
- ¼ cup crumbled Kaserri cheese

Combine all of the ingredients together in a large mixing bowl. Mix well. Knead well. Form a loaf shape. Place on a greased 9 X 13 pan. Put in a cold oven and let rise. This takes about 30 to 45 minutes. Set oven to 400 degrees and bake for about 30 minutes or until golden brown.

COOKING NOTES:

Greek Cheese Pastry—Tyropita

- 3 ¼ tablespoons butter
- 1 tablespoon butter
- 1 ¼ pound crumbled Greek Feta Cheese
- 1 cup milk
- salt to taste
- pepper to taste
- 11/8 cup of oregano
- 1 ¼ pound crumbled Kasseri Cheese
- 5 beaten eggs
- 1 ¼ pounds Filo

Combine all of the ingredients together in a mixing bowl. Mix well. Grease a 9 X 13 pan well. Put approximately half of the Filo sheets on the pan. Put the mixture on top of the half of Filo sheets. On top of the mixture place the remaining Filo sheets. Set oven to 325 degrees and Bake in oven for 45 minutes or until golden light brown/white.

COOKING NOTES:

Greek Cheese Snack

- 1 cup crumbled kefaloteeree Cheese
- 1 cup crumbled Feta Cheese
- 1 cup crumbled Kasseri cheese
- ¼ cup minced garlic
- 1 dozen frozen cup shells
- 2 beaten eggs
- 1 teaspoon water
- ¼ cup dill weed

Mix all the ingredient in a mixing bowl. Mix well for best Greek taste. Take the cup shells and place them on a 9 X 13 greased pan. Take the mixture and place into each shell. Put oven to 350 degrees and bake for about 20 minutes or until golden brown.

COOKING NOTES:

Greek Spinach Pastry

- 3 ¼ cups of flour
- ½ cup of butter
- 1/8 cup of Red Wine Vinegar
- ½ cup of bottled water
- 1 packet self rising yeast
- 1/8 cup Greek white wine

Combine all the ingredients together until a doughy mixture occurs. Knead well. Put in a greased 9 X 13 pan and place in a cold oven for 45 minutes. Remove dough from oven. Semi-flatten the dough and place the stuffing recipe located in this book titled "Greek Spinach Pastry-Stuffing" on the dough. Fold the dough over the stuffing. Set oven at 325 degrees for 45 minutes or until golden brown.

COOKING NOTES:

Greek Spinach Pastry Stuffing

- 4 cups of fresh spinach
- 1 cup of Crumbled Feta Cheese
- 1 ¼ cup of butter
- ½ cup chopped onions
- ¼ cup of oregano

1 cup of Kaserri cheese
salt to taste
pepper to taste
1 ¼ pound turkey breast

Boil the cleaned spinach and cleaned onions for about 15 minutes with small boiling bubbles (low heat). Combine all of the ingredients together in a mixing bowl. Mix well. Utilize this stuffing in the "Greek Spinach Pastry" recipe in this book.

COOKING NOTES:

Greek Moussaka

1 ¼ cup chopped onions
2 lbs. ground lamb
½ cup chopped tomatoes
¼ cup dill weed
8 oz tomato paste
salt to taste
pepper to taste
1 cup extra virgin olive oil
1 cup butter
1 cup flour
3 ¾ cups milk
2 large eggplants
4 medium sized peeled sliced potatoes
1 cup crumbled Feta Cheese

Cook ground lamb until brown any method you ordinarily use. Cook eggplant any method you ordinarily use. Mix all of the ingredients tighter in a large mixing bowl and mix well. Put into a large, greased baking pan. Bake at 325 degrees for 1 hour or until golden brown.

COOKING NOTES:

Greek Fish Soup—Kaakaaviaa Soopau

1 whole sea bass fish
1 ¼ cup Extra Virgin Olive Oil
1 cup chopped onions
2 cups bottled water
½ cup Feta Cheese
1 cup chopped tomatoes
salt to taste
pepper to taste
¼ cup oregano
½ cup Kasseri cheese

Combine all of the ingredients in a tall pan. Bring to a boil and boil low bubbles for about ¾ hour. Remove from heat. Pull out the sea bass fish. Now remove the bones, head, skin, and tail. Put sea bass back into the soup. Soup is now complete and ready to serve.

COOKING NOTES:

Gregory's Greek Salad Dressing

½ Cup Red Wine Vinegar
1 cup of Greek Extra Virgin Olive Oil
¼ cup Dill Weed
½ cup crumbled Greek Feta Cheese
1/8 cup Greek Sea Salt
1/8 cup Fresh Ground Pepper
1/8 cup minced Garlic

Combine in a large measuring cup with a spout to pour. Mix very well and pour generously onto any salad. Enjoy on any salad.

COOKING NOTES:

Index

Macedonian Recipes Section

Greek Recipies Section

CPSIA information can be obtained at www.ICGtesting.com
Printed in the USA
LVOW092032251111

256469LV00003B/59/P